Meet the Megalodon

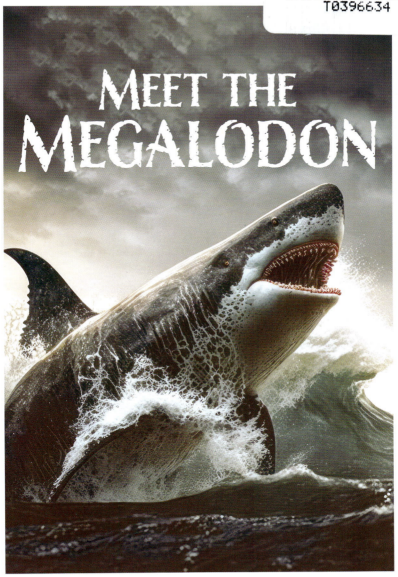

Eric Braun, M.F.A.

Consultants

Matthew T. Miller
Museum Specialist
National Museum of Natural History

Cheryl Lane, M.Ed.
Seventh Grade Science Teacher
Chino Valley Unified School District

Michelle Wertman, M.S.Ed.
Literacy Specialist
New York City Public Schools

Publishing Credits

Rachelle Cracchiolo, M.S.Ed., *Publisher*
Emily R. Smith, M.A.Ed., *SVP of Content Development*
Véronique Bos, *VP of Creative*
Dani Neiley, *Editor*
Robin Erickson, *Senior Art Director*

Smithsonian Enterprises

Avery Naughton, *Licensing Coordinator*
Paige Towler, *Editorial Lead*
Jill Corcoran, *Senior Director, Licensed Publishing*
Brigid Ferraro, *Vice President of New Business and Licensing*
Carol LeBlanc, *President*

Image Credits: p.5 Alamy Stock Photo; p.6 Millard H. Sharp/Science Source; p.10 JA CHIRINOS/Science Source; p.17 Alamy Stock Photo; p.18 Smithsonian Institution; p.19 MASATO HATTORI/Science Source; p.23 Chris Hellier/Science Source; ; all other images from iStock and/or Shutterstock, or in the public domain

Library of Congress Cataloging in Publication Control Number: 2024024236

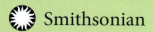

© 2025 Smithsonian Institution. The name "Smithsonian" and the Smithsonian logo are registered trademarks owned by the Smithsonian Institution.

This book may not be reproduced or distributed in any way without prior written consent from the publisher.

5482 Argosy Avenue
Huntington Beach, CA 92649
www.tcmpub.com
ISBN 979-8-7659-6864-2
© 2025 Teacher Created Materials, Inc.
Printed by: 51497
Printed in : China

Table of Contents

Toothy Titans..................4

Prehistoric Predators..............6

Mysterious Discoveries...........12

Millions of Years of Evolution.......18

What Happened to Megalodon?....22

Appetite for Imagination..........26

STEAM Challenge...............28

Glossary.......................30

Index.........................31

Career Advice..................32

Toothy Titans

Imagine coming face-to-face with a massive, mega-toothed shark. This creature is 16 meters (52 feet) long, almost twice as large as a killer whale. It looks down at you with a mouth that is 3 meters (10 feet) wide, big enough to devour you and some of your friends. And just get a glimpse of those teeth. Each one has sharp, jagged edges and is the size of an adult's hand.

This giant fish is a species of shark called *Otodus megalodon*. People usually call these sharks "megalodon." (Fun fact: the word *megalodon* is both singular and plural.) You can see one in person at the National Museum of Natural History in Washington, DC. But it's just a model. It was installed at the museum in 2019.

Megalodon have been **extinct** for millions of years, but in their time, they were some of the fiercest **predators** to ever live. They were the top predators of their time, chowing down on whales, seals, and everything else below them in the food chain.

FUN FACT

The word *megalodon* comes from two Greek words. When translated, those two words mean "giant tooth." Considering the size of their teeth, their name fits them well!

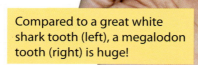

Compared to a great white shark tooth (left), a megalodon tooth (right) is huge!

Scientists called ***paleontologists*** have learned about megalodon by studying their fossils. Scientists have discovered how megalodon lived, how they **evolved**, and how they went extinct. There's a lot to unpack about these sharks, so let's dive in!

Museum workers assemble a megalodon model.

Prehistoric Predators

Did you know that sharks have been on Earth for 400 million years? Just like the oceans today, **prehistoric** waters contained different types of sharks. Scientists know this thanks to the **fossil record**.

Megalodon were prehistoric sharks. They first appeared on Earth about 23 million years ago and died out about 3.6 million years ago. During those years, these sharks lived in all the oceans. While they did sometimes swim in deep areas of oceans, they preferred to roam coastal areas. They could even live in smaller **marine** areas, such as lagoons, lakes, and rivers.

Scientists use fossils, like this jaw and teeth from a giant scissor shark, to learn more about prehistoric sharks.

Some prehistoric sharks had teeth that grew in curved clusters.

For many years, megalodon have been a fascinating topic for scientists. In the 1800s, a scientist named Louis Agassiz was the first person to describe them. He believed they were related to great white sharks. That's because both species have similar looking, **serrated** teeth. Over time, scientists have debated how to **classify** megalodon. Today, they are classified separately from great whites. Scientists believe that they are in a different family, which is a collection of many species. They think great white sharks lived alongside megalodon until megalodon became extinct.

What Did They Look Like?

Without seeing megalodon in the flesh, no one can know exactly what they looked like. But, thanks to fossils, scientists have some good ideas.

Scientists estimate that megalodon were the largest sharks to ever live. They could grow to be about 16 meters (52 feet) long. That's almost as big as a semi-truck and its trailer. Megalodon were roughly three times bigger than great white sharks and twice as big as orcas. Megalodon likely weighed up to 45 metric tons (50 tons). And newborn megalodon may have been about 2 meters (6.6 feet) long. That is longer than the height of an average adult male!

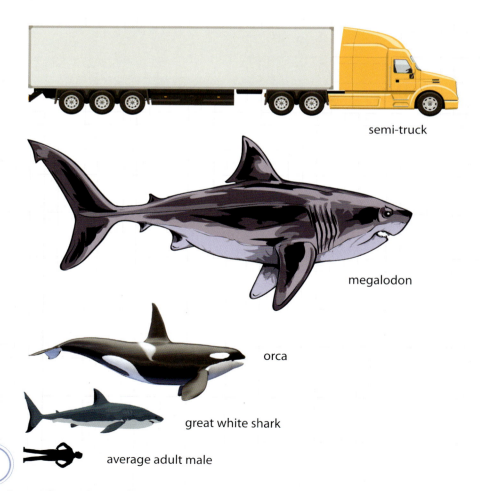

semi-truck

megalodon

orca

great white shark

average adult male

Megalodon shared some physical similarities with other sharks. They had powerful, **streamlined** bodies. Their bodies allowed them to move through the water quickly and easily. Beneath their skin, their skeletons were made mostly of **cartilage**. That's the same material that makes up your nose and ears. Megalodon were also able to swim long distances without getting too tired.

The most striking feature of megalodon were their mouths. Scientists think that each of their jaws held about 276 teeth. Their mouths could be up to 3 meters (11 feet) wide. Compared to great white sharks, megalodon had shorter noses and flatter jaws. They continuously shed their teeth as they wore out and grew new ones.

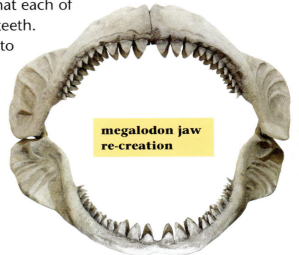

megalodon jaw re-creation

TECHNOLOGY

Computer Modeling

In 2022, scientists used part of a backbone fossil to create the first 3D model of megalodon. With this model, they visualized how megalodon might have looked. They also estimated how they moved and how fast they swam.

Time to Eat!

Megalodon were apex predators in the oceans. They had a position at the top of the food chain. They could hunt other fish without being hunted themselves. Megalodon were meat eaters, or carnivores. As they swam through the water, their **prey** were no match for their power and speed.

Megalodon had healthy appetites, and they ate a variety of fish and mammals in the water. They were big enough to eat large fish, dolphins, and other sharks. They could swallow some of these creatures whole. But megalodon did not only go after bite-sized meals. Larger sea creatures, including ancient whales, were their prey, too. Ancient whales could be more than 15 meters (50 feet) long—roughly the same length as megalodon!

No photographs of megalodon exist, so artists depict how they might have hunted ancient whales.

How did megalodon take down such large animals? The answer lies in their powerful jaws and sharp, serrated teeth, which were able to tear flesh to shreds. Scientists estimate that megalodon had up to 10 times the bite strength of great white sharks. With this combination of extremely sharp teeth and strength, animals of any size were possible prey for megalodon. Megalodon might have first attacked larger animals by taking large bites out of their bodies and waiting for them to die. Then, they could finish eating their prey.

Megalodon teeth and great white shark teeth have similar edges.

SCIENCE

Strong Swimmers

Scientists believe that megalodon were high-speed swimmers. They think that megalodon could cruise at a faster speed than any sharks alive today. In 2022, some scientists estimated an average cruising rate of 1.4 meters (4.6 feet) per second.

Mysterious Discoveries

People have found shark teeth, including megalodon teeth, since ancient times. When people first found these strange objects on land, they didn't know what they were. Around 70 CE, a Roman philosopher named Pliny the Elder guessed that shark teeth were meteorites. He thought they fell to Earth during lunar eclipses.

Pliny the Elder

Fast forward to the Middle Ages (500–1500 CE). During this time, people believed that shark teeth were the tongues of dragons or snakes that had been turned into stone. They called them *tongue stones*. People believed they had magical and medicinal powers. Tongue stones were seen as an antidote to snake bites and poison. Tongue stones were thought to be cures for plagues, fevers, and other conditions. People even believed that tongue stones could cure bad breath. For these reasons, tongue stones were considered very valuable. People wore them as jewelry or sewed them into their pockets.

Shark teeth are still used in some modern jewelry.

People have been finding and studying megalodon teeth for hundreds of years.

In 1666, an Italian fisherman caught a great white shark. The shark's head was sent to a scientist named Nicolas Steno. Steno saw that the shark's teeth looked a lot like tongue stones. He was the first person to realize that tongue stones were actually fossils. Around this same time, early scientists began to recognize that fossils were **preserved** remains of prehistoric life.

Fossils of ancient animals like dinosaurs have been found all over the world.

Dig into Fossils

Fossil formation is extremely rare. A specific set of conditions needs to be met so they can form. An exact amount of pressure, heat, and **sediment** has to be applied to an organism's remains. Plus, the right length of time needs to go by—at least 10,000 years! Fossils of bugs, plants, animals, and even animal footprints have been found around the world. Luckily, scientists have found megalodon fossils, too.

Megalodon teeth have been found on every continent except Antarctica. In North America, scientists have found some megalodon bones along the coasts and in certain rivers. Most megalodon fossils are teeth or **vertebrae**. So far, no full skeletons of megalodon have been found. That's because their skeletons were made of cartilage, which is softer than bone. Cartilage does not hold up well in fossil formation. However, the fossils scientists do have give them a glimpse into the lives of these ancient sharks.

Through fossils, paleontologists can learn more about how megalodon lived. Fossilized teeth give clues as to how big these sharks were. Scientists can use the size of their teeth to estimate the size of the rest of their mouths. They can infer that these sharks were meat eaters who tore into their prey. And scientists have even found evidence of megalodon on other fossils. Some fossilized whale bones have cut marks on them. These cuts match megalodon teeth.

Most of what scientists have learned about megalodon is based on fossils of their teeth.

FUN FACT

In the summer of 2022, a diver in North Carolina found several megalodon teeth. One was 15 centimeters (6 inches) long! That's nearly as long as a one-dollar bill.

Making Models

For more than a century, scientists wanted to figure out exactly how big megalodon were. One way they approached this was by building models. Using fossils to create models of megalodon has been a lengthy process.

In 1909, a scientist named Bashford Dean built the first physical megalodon model. He created a model of a jaw by using what he learned from fossilized megalodon teeth. Dean used the jaw of a great white shark to figure out megalodon **proportions**. At the time, scientists thought these sharks were related. For the final touch on Dean's model, he lined it with real teeth. Dean's model was displayed in a famous museum in New York City. Based on his model, scientists of the time thought that megalodon could grow up to 30 meters (100 feet) long.

MATHEMATICS

How Big?

In 2020, a group of scientists used mathematics to find out more about the size of megalodon. To do this, they took measurements of four other species of sharks. After working with these numbers, they came up with head, fin, and tail measurements. One of their findings was that megalodon tails were roughly 3.85 meters (12.6 feet) long.

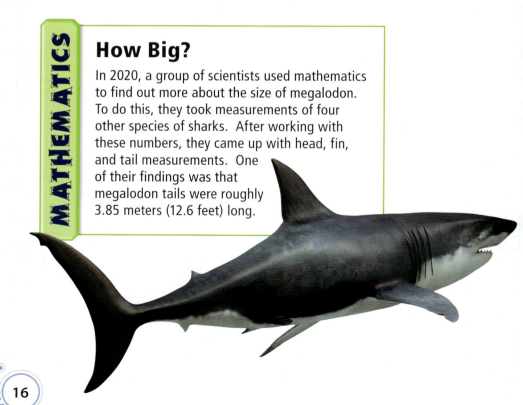

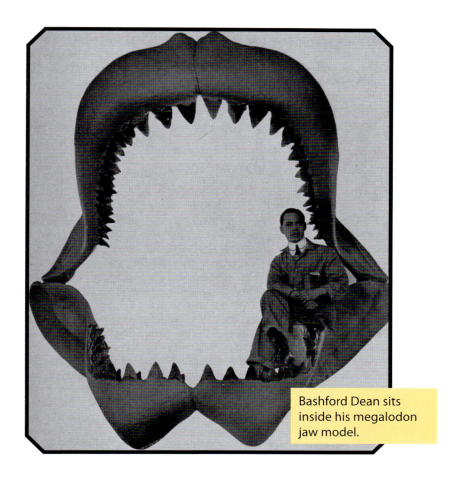

Bashford Dean sits inside his megalodon jaw model.

In the 1980s, scientists figured out that Dean's model was too big. The Smithsonian Institution hired a paleontologist named John Maisey to construct another model. They wanted to create a model with more accuracy. Maisey used recently found megalodon teeth to make a more authentic comparison to great white sharks. And in 1985, the more accurate model went on display. It was roughly two-thirds the size of Dean's model.

Scientists continue to learn more about megalodon based on fossils. Thanks to advances in technology, they can now build models on computers. And as more fossils are found, more research can be done.

Millions of Years of Evolution

About 420 million years ago, Earth looked very different compared to how it does today. On land, there were no trees. In fact, the first plants were just starting to grow. In the oceans, shelled squid-like animals were the top predators. The first fish were just beginning to evolve. Ancient ancestors of spiders and horseshoe crabs scampered across the ocean floor.

Around this time, the earliest known shark-like fish appeared. These fish had skulls and jaws that made them look somewhat similar to modern sharks. And like modern sharks, their skeletons were made of cartilage. Over millions of years, more and more of these fish roamed the seas. By about 360 million years ago, sharks dominated the food chain.

As sharks evolved over the next 200 million years, they formed new adaptations. They were able to swim faster. They developed flexible jaws, making it easier for them to sink their teeth into their prey. About 103 million years ago, a new group of sharks evolved. Their scientific name is *Cretalamna*. Scientists determined that these sharks were a direct ancestor of megalodon. Their teeth were very similar to megalodon. And all these sharks were very fast swimmers.

fossilized teeth of *Cretalamna* sharks

This is what scientists think underwater life on Earth looked like between 444 and 419 million years ago.

Let's jump to about 66 million years ago. Around this time, a giant asteroid struck Earth. The impact caused widespread devastation that killed most living things on the planet. Among sharks, most of the smallest, bottom-dwelling species survived. The sharks that were left had little competition for prey. So, they were able to hunt freely. Millions of years later, marine mammals, such as whales, began to appear. Over the next several million years, whales got bigger. So did the sharks that hunted them.

About 40 million years ago, another new group of sharks evolved. Their scientific name is *Otodus*. This group was related to *Cretalamna* sharks. Sharks in this group could grow up to 10 meters (33 feet) long. Their teeth reached a maximum size of about 10 centimeters (4 inches). Over millions of years, these sharks grew larger still. Their teeth evolved to be wider and serrated. By about 23 million years ago, these sharks had evolved into what we now know as megalodon. They were the largest, fastest ocean predators of all time.

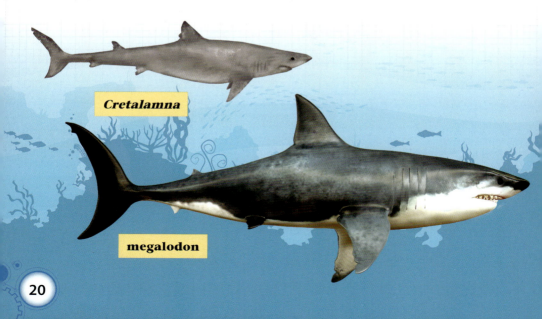

Cretalamna

megalodon

Some modern sharks share similarities with megalodon, including great white sharks. But the closest modern relative to megalodon are mako sharks. Mako sharks have streamlined bodies just like megalodon did, and they are also very fast.

shortfin mako shark

great white shark

What Happened to Megalodon?

It might sound exciting to see live megalodon, but this will never happen. No megalodon are still alive on Earth. They stopped showing up in the fossil record long ago. Scientists have a couple of estimates for when this happened.

Before 2019, some scientists thought megalodon became extinct 2.6 million years ago. This was around the same time as a supernova, which is the explosion of a star. Harmful debris from the supernova fell to Earth. This killed many species, including megalodon. Scientists also had dated some megalodon fossils and found they were 2.6 million years old. So, the timing matched up.

However, a study from 2019 led to a different extinction estimate. Scientists estimated it at 3.6 million years ago. And today, most of the scientific community agrees with this date. Scientists got this number by testing the ages of megalodon fossils from all over the world. The testing methods they used were more precise than previous methods. So, the ages of these fossils were more accurate. Scientists also learned that some fossils dated by the previous researchers had been dated wrong. Some of them were not even megalodon fossils.

ENGINEERING

Back to Life

Some people wonder if megalodon **DNA** could be used to bring them back from extinction. That's because DNA can sometimes be found in well-preserved teeth. However, scientists know that this is not possible. DNA is simply too fragile. It does not hold up well over millions of years.

Museums around the world display re-creations of megalodon fossils to give the public a glimpse into the past.

Studying ancient life is a difficult task. It is hard to get exact answers from fragile fossils, especially when they are millions of years old. But advances in technology can lead to new discoveries. Scientists will likely discover more about megalodon in years to come.

We have an estimate of when megalodon died out. But do we know how? What happened to megalodon, anyway? Again, it's hard to know for sure. However, scientists do have some theories on why these sharks disappeared from the fossil record.

Around the time megalodon died, Earth's **climate** changed drastically. The oceans began to cool down a lot. And megalodon liked warm water. Remember how megalodon fossils have been found all over the world? That's because the world's oceans were very warm. But as the water turned cold and icy, megalodon would have lost huge areas of their habitat.

Scientists think the changing climate may have led to a steep drop in available prey. Like megalodon, many marine animals at the time were used to warmer water. So, some of them began to die out in the colder water. Others may have adapted and found different places to live in the colder waters. At this point, megalodon had less habitat *and* less food. Things were not looking good.

Climate change in the past involved an ice age, and the planet's climate went from warm to cold.

Great white sharks have always been fierce predators.

A final factor in their demise may have been the evolution of great white sharks. The diet of a great white shark overlapped significantly with the diet of megalodon. Megalodon were used to being the top predators. But now, they had serious competition when it came to hunting prey.

FUN FACT

Whales and other mammals evolved to have a special ability in cold water. These animals could regulate their body temperatures. Scientists think that megalodon could also do this. But when the water became super cold, this process required too much energy from megalodon. They could not survive the brutal cold.

Ancient whales adapted to the cold water.

Appetite for Imagination

Scientists will continue to study fossils and learn more about ancient creatures, including megalodon. This work can help them understand how ancient life roamed the planet.

Megalodon have not only fascinated scientists. These giant sharks have captured the imaginations of all kinds of people. How could they not? They were the largest marine predators that we know of. People have gobbled up stories about megalodon, just as megalodon once gobbled up their prey. You can find many documentaries about these sharks. Fictional books and movies have been made, too.

Oceans cover about 71 percent of our planet. And only a small amount of that has been explored. So, some people believe that megalodon are still alive out there. After all, nobody can easily see what is in the deepest, darkest parts of our oceans. But megalodon really are gone. They became extinct long ago.

Still, megalodon capture our imaginations. We wonder what it would have been like to see them in their natural habitats. Fossils are rare puzzle pieces that help create a full picture of megalodon. And one thing is for sure—we've never seen predators like these sharks before.

ARTS

Lights, Camera, Action!

In 2018, filmmakers brought megalodon to life on the big screen. *The Meg* is loosely based on a science-fiction novel. The story follows a group of scientists who encounter one of these sharks.

STEAM CHALLENGE

Define the Problem

Paleontologists dig deep to uncover clues about Earth's history. They visit sites and use tools to find all types of fossils. Your task is to design and build a sifting tool to help them look for fossils and ancient artifacts. Your tool must allow space for sand and sediment to move through while holding onto larger objects, such as shells and rocks.

Constraints: You may only use the materials provided to you.

Criteria: Your sifting tool must be able to collect at least five larger objects from a sand sample. The tool must also allow sand and sediment to move through.

Research and Brainstorm
What types of fossils do paleontologists search for? What do they learn from studying fossils?

Design and Build
Sketch two or more designs for your sifting tool. Label the parts and materials. Choose the design you think will work best. Then, build your sifting tool.

Test and Improve
Share your sifter with others. Demonstrate how your tool works by using it to collect larger items while allowing sand and small particles to move through. Point out key features on your sifter. How can you improve it? Will you set any new goals for your design? What are they? Modify your design and reassess how well it meets the criteria.

Reflect and Share
What about this challenge did you find most interesting? How could you modify your design so that it will be able to collect smaller items? What did you learn that you could apply to other challenges?

Glossary

cartilage—a somewhat flexible, lightweight tissue that gives structural support in sharks' skeletons and can be found in human ears and noses

classify—to arrange a group of animals into categories according to their similarities

climate—the weather patterns of a place or region over a long period of time

DNA—the information inside the cells of living things that acts like instructions for how to make that organism's body; abbreviation for deoxyribonucleic acid

evolved—(regarding species) developed and changed gradually over time

extinct—no longer existing

fossil record—a log of all documented fossils that shows the history of life

marine—of or relating to the sea

paleontologists—experts who study fossil remains of animals and plants

predators—animals that get food by hunting other animals

prehistoric—of, relating to, or existing in times before written history

preserved—protected and kept safe from damage

prey—an animal or animals that are hunted by predators for food

proportions—the sizes, numbers, or amounts of one thing or group as compared to the sizes, numbers, or amounts of another thing or group

sediment—solid material (such as stones and sand) deposited by water, wind, or glaciers

serrated—jagged, saw-like edge

streamlined—shaped in a way that allows for smooth movement through water or air

vertebrae—small bones that form the backbone of an organism

Index

Antarctica, 14

cartilage, 9, 14, 18

climate, 24

Cretalamna, 18, 20

Dean, Bashford, 16–17

fossils, 5–6, 8–9, 13–14, 16–17, 22–24, 26–27

great white sharks, 4, 7–9, 11, 13, 16–17, 21, 25

jaws, 6, 9, 11, 16–18

Maisey, John, 17

mako sharks, 21

mammals, 10, 20, 25

Meg, The, 27

Middle Ages, 12

North America, 14

North Carolina, 15

Otodus, 4, 20

paleontologists, 5, 14, 17

Pliny the Elder, 12

predators, 4, 6, 10, 18, 20, 25–27

prey, 10–11, 14, 18, 20, 24–26

sediment, 14

Steno, Nicolas, 13

teeth, 4, 6–7, 9, 11–18, 20, 22

tongue stones, 12–13

whales, 4, 10, 14, 20, 25

CAREER ADVICE
from Smithsonian

Do you want to study ancient life?

Here are some tips to keep in mind for the future.

"Why do horses have four legs, but people have two? What was Earth like before insects existed? When did the first predator eat its first prey? Paleontologists try to answer questions like these because they are curious about the history of life more than any other topic. If this sounds like you, keep feeding your curiosity! Take all the geology and biology classes that you can. Keep reading, always ask questions, and never stop learning."

– Kathy Hollis, Collections Manager, Department of Paleobiology, National Museum of Natural History

"Becoming a paleontologist requires solid training in biology and geology. In college, aspiring paleontologists usually major in either field but should take courses in the other. It is important for students to go out into the field with experienced people who will teach them how to recognize, document, and collect fossils. Most jobs in paleontology now require graduate training."

– Dr. Hans Sues, Senior Research Geologist and Curator of Vertebrate Paleontology, Department of Paleobiology, National Museum of Natural History